PRAY 20 jOurnal

Timothy Eldred
with Brian Smith

CHRISTIAN ENDEAVOR INTERNATIONAL

PRAY21 JOURNAL
© 2007 Christian Endeavor International
International Standard Book Number: 978-0-9796551-1-1

Cover design by Zeal
Interior design and typeset by Katherine Lloyd, The DESK

Printed in Canada

For information:
Christian Endeavor International
PO Box 377
424 East Main Street
Edmore, MI 48829

Contents

Journaling the Journey

You're an author! Just by living, following Jesus, you're writing a story. It's a sequel to the one Jesus started two thousand years ago.

Jesus came in the flesh to launch a miraculous mission…an earthshaking, world-rescue mission. After he returned to heaven, he came back to live inside people. Since then, Jesus has continued his earthshaking, world-rescue mission…through his followers. Through you.

This book is one place where you can save part of your story on paper—it might prove to be valuable reading later. But even if you never read it again, the act of writing something down has a way of solidifying it in our minds, making it more real.

This *Journal* is also a tool to help you remember thoughts and commitments from your discussions with your partners. And when you make discoveries on your own, you can write them here to share in your next meeting.

The 21 entries in this *Journal* correspond to the 21 daily readings in the *Pray21 Discovery Guide*. Each entry includes a few additional thoughts from God to you, along with a generous allotment of white space for you to write your responses to questions, your prayers, and anything else you want. Even unanswered questions you'd still like to figure out.

Live the Jesus life. Fill out a little more of the Jesus story. And use this *Journal* to help you process and remember what you're learning along the way. This is a journey worth remembering.

how many loaves
do you have?

Remember, dear brothers and sisters, that few of you were wise in the world's eyes or powerful or wealthy when God called you. Instead, God chose things the world considers foolish in order to shame those who think they are wise. And he chose things that are powerless to shame those who are powerful. God chose things despised by the world, things counted as nothing at all, and used them to bring to nothing what the world considers important. As a result, no one can ever boast in the presence of God.... Therefore, as the Scriptures say, "If you want to boast, boast only about the LORD."

1 CORINTHIANS 1:26–29, 31, NLT

Whoever can be trusted with very little can also be trusted with much.

LUKE 16:10, NIV

You may not think you have much to offer God, but all he wants is all you have. Bring it to him, and watch it multiply in his hands.

BRIEF DEBRIEF

You can use the space below to take notes if you're discussing these questions with your partners. If, instead, you're working through the questions alone, you can write your thoughts, commitments, and prayers, and bring them to share next time you meet.

• What tempts you to think that you don't have
what it takes to accomplish God's mission?

What do you wish you could do for
God and others, but are afraid to do?

What thoughts and emotions do you wrestle with?

• How many loaves *do* you have? (Be honest.)

How might God honor your small-seeming gift?

• What is he asking you to do for him or others this week?

Why will this be of value?

• What will you bring to him, for his use?

• What support or resources do
you need from others this week?

What do they need from you?

"Lord, you're amazing. I bring you
everything I have, and you always
multiply my few loaves into a feast
for thousands."
                    —Philip's story
        Day 1, PRAY21 DISCOVERY GUIDE

SECURE CHANNEL

Here's space for you to "pray on paper," writing out your conversation with God about bringing all you have to him.

Prayer for myself:

Prayer for my partners (or others):

LOOSE ENDS

As you were reading, thinking, and praying today, did any questions come to mind that were left unanswered? Write them here, so you can ask your partners or research them later on your own.

do you really believe I can do this?

I tell you the truth, anyone who has faith in me will do what I have been doing. He will do even greater things than these, because I am going to the Father. And I will do whatever you ask in my name, so that the Son may bring glory to the Father. You may ask me for anything in my name, and I will do it.

JOHN 14:12–14, NIV

God…creates each of us by Christ Jesus to join him in the work he does, the good work he has gotten ready for us to do, work we had better be doing.

EPHESIANS 2:10

I ask [the Father] to strengthen you by his Spirit—not a brute strength but a glorious inner strength.

EPHESIANS 3:16

•———————•

God wants you to live his dream. But that means taking *him* seriously. How big do you think he really is? And it means taking *yourself* seriously. Will you dream big with God, and then actively participate in your own dream?

BRIEF DEBRIEF

In the space below, dream big with your partners if you're doing this together. Or dream your own dreams alone with God, write them down, and share them next time you meet.

- "What do you want me to do for you?" What's
  your dream for God, for changing the world?

- "Do you really believe I can do this?" How big
  is your God? Big enough for your dream?

Zach wanted to be the seed, one
gram of yeast, and let God change
the world through him.

—Zach Hunter's story
Day 2, PRAY21 DISCOVERY GUIDE

- If you haven't already, turn your dream into a request. Step up to the throne and petition the King to make it happen.

- What will be your first step in living the dream?

- Who else do you need to dream and live it with you?

SECURE CHANNEL

Here you can write whatever crosses your mind as you brainstorm *huge* with God.

Prayer for myself:

_____

_____

_____

_____

_____

_____

_____

Prayer for my partners (or others):

_____

_____

_____

_____

_____

LOOSE ENDS

As you were reading, thinking, and praying today, did any questions come to mind that were left unanswered? Write them here, so you can ask your partners or research them later on your own.

do you believe
in the Son?

God sacrificed Jesus on the altar of the world to clear that world of sin. Having faith in him sets us in the clear. God decided on this course of action in full view of the public—to set the world in the clear with himself through the sacrifice of Jesus, finally taking care of the sins he had so patiently endured.

ROMANS 3:25

Immense in mercy and with an incredible love, [God] embraced us. He took our sin-dead lives and made us alive in Christ. He did all this on his own, with no help from us! Then he picked us up and set us down in highest heaven in company with Jesus, our Messiah.

EPHESIANS 2:4–6

[God] has given us eternal life, and this life is in his Son. Whoever has the Son has life; whoever does not have God's Son does not have life. I have written this to you who believe in the name of the Son of God, so that you may know you have eternal life. And we are confident that he hears us whenever we ask for anything that pleases him. And since we know he hears us when we make our requests, we also know that he will give us what we ask for.

1 JOHN 5:11–15, NLT

The miracle life begins with a miracle relationship. Have you become God's son or daughter through Jesus' sacrifice for you? If you have, are you living the passionate miracle life your Father has planned for you?

BRIEF DEBRIEF

Use this space either to take notes while discussing these questions with your partners, or to write your personal thoughts to share with them later. You're dealing here with the most important relationship in your life, so be honest with yourself, God, and your friends.

• What's the difference between knowing Jesus and knowing *about* him?

• What's the difference between knowing Jesus and doing the good things he says to do?

"If the gospel weren't true, I'd thank God to annihilate me this instant. I wouldn't want to live if you could destroy the name of Jesus Christ."[1] —Charles Spurgeon quote
Day 3, PRAY21 DISCOVERY GUIDE

- If someone asked you how to start a relationship with Jesus, what would you say?

- Do you know the Son of Man? You can pray to him now, using the following prayer or any words that convey the same ideas. Then you'll have his presence in you, helping you live the life you've always really wanted.

  Jesus, I've done wrong things, and I don't deserve forgiveness or heaven. Thank you for dying for me. I accept your forgiveness, your free gift of eternal life. Change me inside, and help me live for you. Thank you for this miracle in me. Now do miracles through me.

SECURE CHANNEL

Feel free to write your thoughts to God (and his thoughts to you) about your miracle relationship with Jesus and the miracle life you can be living.

Prayer for myself:

Prayer for my partners (or others):

LOOSE ENDS

As you were reading, thinking, and praying today, did any questions come to mind that were left unanswered? Write them here, so you can ask your partners or research them later on your own.

why did you doubt?

*Be strong and very courageous. Be careful to obey all [God's instructions].
Do not deviate from them, turning either to the right or to the left. Then
you will be successful in everything you do. Study this Book of Instruction
continually. Meditate on it day and night so you will be sure to obey
everything written in it. Only then will you prosper and succeed in all you
do. This is my command—be strong and courageous! Do not be afraid or
discouraged. For the Lord your God is with you wherever you go.*

JOSHUA 1:7–9, NLT

*[Don't] worry about everyday life—whether you have enough food and
drink, or enough clothes to wear. Isn't life more than food, and your body
more than clothing?... Can all your worries add a single moment to your
life?... So don't worry about these things, saying, "What will we eat? What
will we drink? What will we wear?" These things dominate the thoughts of
unbelievers, but your heavenly Father already knows all your needs. Seek
the Kingdom of God above all else, and live righteously, and he will give
you everything you need.*

MATTHEW 6:25, 27, 31–33, NLT

God understands our doubts...up to a point. But he loses patience when
we keep hiding in doubts, because he knows how much we can accomplish when we break through and trust him.

BRIEF DEBRIEF

Below you can write your thoughts—either privately or with
your partners—about your dealings with doubt. Even if you
work through these questions alone, don't try to battle doubt all by yourself. Connect with someone you trust to go alongside you.

• Describe one doubt that makes it
  hard for you to trust and obey God.

• What helps you beat it?

What makes it worse?

Doubt flooded her, and she kept
pouring it into God's hands. Finally
he helped her escape doubt's tyr-
anny. Doubt became a choice, and she
rejected it.   —Esther's story
              Day 4, PRAY21 DISCOVERY GUIDE

DAY 4

- How do you need people? _____

_____

_____

_____

_____

_____

_____

What can we do for you?

_____

_____

_____

_____

_____

_____

- Don't wait for fear to disappear. Fear isn't the opposite of faith.
  Disobedience is. What step will you take _____
  to show faith in spite of fear this week? _____

_____

_____

_____

_____

_____

_____

Secure Channel

Here's space for you to "pray on paper," writing out your conversation with God about finding courage in the face of doubts.

Prayer for myself:

_____

_____

_____

_____

_____

_____

_____

Prayer for my partners (or others):

_____

_____

_____

_____

_____

_____

Loose Ends

As you were reading, thinking, and praying today, did any questions come to mind that were left unanswered? Write them here, so you can ask your partners or research them later on your own.

don't you know me yet?

Live in me [Jesus]. Make your home in me just as I do in you. In the same way that a branch can't bear grapes by itself but only by being joined to the vine, you can't bear fruit unless you are joined with me. I am the Vine, you are the branches. When you're joined with me and I with you, the relation intimate and organic, the harvest is sure to be abundant. Separated, you can't produce a thing.... But if you make yourselves at home with me and my words are at home in you, you can be sure that whatever you ask will be listened to and acted upon. This is how my Father shows who he is— when you produce grapes, when you mature as my disciples.

JOHN 15:4–8

[When he returns in his glory,] the King will say to those on his right, "Come, you who are blessed by my Father, inherit the Kingdom prepared for you from the creation of the world. For I was hungry, and you fed me. I was thirsty, and you gave me a drink. I was a stranger, and you invited me into your home. I was naked, and you gave me clothing. I was sick, and you cared for me. I was in prison, and you visited me."

Then these righteous ones will reply, "Lord, when did we ever see you hungry and feed you? Or thirsty and give you something to drink? Or a stranger and show you hospitality? Or naked and give you clothing? When did we ever see you sick or in prison and visit you?"

And the King will say, "I tell you the truth, when you did it to one of the least of these my brothers and sisters, you were doing it to me!"

MATTHEW 25:34–40, NLT

How long have you been with Jesus? Any time with him is time to get to know him. In person. Open your eyes. He's everywhere in your life. Open your ears. He's talking to you. Open your heart, let him in close...and watch out, world!

BRIEF DEBRIEF

Jesus is right there with you when you're working through these questions—alone or with your partners. Absorb the love, power, and truth of his Presence. Think about the difference his actual presence makes in your responses here.

- What are some ways you've seen and come to know Jesus personally in your time with him?

- What difference has this vision of him made in your attitudes and way of living?

DAY 5

- In what ways do you need to open your eyes to Jesus, take a fresh look at him, revive your relationship with him?

- What's one step you'll take now to see and know Jesus better?

Ruby saw Jesus with a child's wide-open eyes. So by the time she needed him most, she knew him well enough to brave challenges that would take many of us down. —Ruby Bridges's story
Day 5, PRAY21 DISCOVERY GUIDE

Secure Channel

Take a few notes on your conversation with God about gaining and maintaining a clearer vision of Jesus.

Prayer for myself:

Prayer for my partners (or others):

Loose Ends

As you were reading, thinking, and praying today, did any questions come to mind that were left unanswered? Write them here, so you can ask your partners or research them later on your own.

haven't I handpicked you?

Long before he laid down earth's foundations, [God] had us in mind, had settled on us as the focus of his love, to be made whole and holy by his love. Long, long ago he decided to adopt us into his family through Jesus Christ. (What pleasure he took in planning this!) He wanted us to enter into the celebration of his lavish gift-giving by the hand of his beloved Son....

Long before we first heard of Christ and got our hopes up, he had his eye on us, had designs on us for glorious living, part of the overall purpose he is working out in everything and everyone. It's in Christ that you, once you heard the truth and believed it (this Message of your salvation), found yourselves home free—signed, sealed, and delivered by the Holy Spirit. This signet from God is the first installment on what's coming, a reminder that we'll get everything God has planned for us, a praising and glorious life.

EPHESIANS 1:4–6, 11–14

[Your unique gifting by God] makes you more significant, not less. A body isn't just a single part blown up into something huge. It's all the different-but-similar parts arranged and functioning together.... God has carefully placed each part of the body right where he wanted it.

1 CORINTHIANS 12:14, 18

[Christ] makes the whole body fit together perfectly. As each part does its own special work, it helps the other parts grow, so that the whole body is healthy and growing and full of love.

EPHESIANS 4:16, NLT

Jesus chose you consciously, with purpose. You weren't forced on him; you weren't his default choice. He wants you. (You have value.) And he has an important mission for you. (You have purpose.) You're handpicked!

BRIEF DEBRIEF

All of us, at times, need to be reassured that we are valuable and that we live for an important reason. While you're wrestling with these questions, invite God and your partners (when you meet) to help you see yourself the way God sees you. He's always right... even about you.

• What do you honestly believe about your worth to God and your special design for his mission?

What are you *told* is true about you, but have a hard time believing?

• What can you do to become more convinced of your value to God?

God loves and treasures each one-of-a-kind child and adult. *On purpose.* He always has.
—Day 6, PRAY21 DISCOVERY GUIDE

- What can you do to become more convinced
  that Jesus wants you on his team, that
  he has an important job for you to do?

- For today, don't work hard at figuring out what your life assignment is.
  Focus on simply believing it exists.
  What's one step you will take toward firmly
  grasping the truth of your value and purpose?

You're valuable as a specialist-on-assignment, intended to carry out a preplanned, you-designed, you-customized, you-nique task in his mission.

—Day 6, PRAY21 DISCOVERY GUIDE

SECURE CHANNEL

Write some of your thoughts—and God's thoughts—about your genuine value and purpose. This may provide an important reminder for you later, when you're feeling worthless and meaningless.

Prayer for myself:

_____

_____

_____

_____

_____

_____

Prayer for my partners (or others):

_____

_____

_____

_____

_____

LOOSE ENDS

As you were reading, thinking, and praying today, did any questions come to mind that were left unanswered? Write them here, so you can ask your partners or research them later on your own.

what good to gain the world and lose your soul?

You are the ones chosen by God, chosen for the high calling of priestly work, chosen to be a holy people, God's instruments to do his work and speak out for him, to tell others of the night-and-day difference he made for you—from nothing to something, from rejected to accepted. Friends, this world is not your home, so don't make yourselves cozy in it. Don't indulge your ego at the expense of your soul. Live an exemplary life among the natives so that your actions will refute their prejudices. Then they'll be won over to God's side and be there to join in the celebration when he arrives.

1 PETER 2:9–12

Each one of these people of faith [Old Testament heroes] died not yet having in hand what was promised, but still believing. How did they do it? They saw it way off in the distance, waved their greeting, and accepted the fact that they were transients in this world. People who live this way make it plain that they are looking for their true home. If they were homesick for the old country, they could have gone back any time they wanted. But they were after a far better country than that—heaven country. You can see why God is so proud of them, and has a City waiting for them.

HEBREWS 11:13–16

————•————

Do you ever feel strange in this life? Maybe it's because you're a stranger here. Earth isn't home for God's kids. But you're not a stranger in heaven, your real home. And you're not a stranger among God's family, your fellow believers. Find strength in these realities to move ahead with your mission on earth, as a friendly foreigner.

BRIEF DEBRIEF

Keep a line open to your heavenly Father, who's with you, and who's also looking forward to your Homecoming some day. Wrestle with these questions on your own or with your partners.

- What are the things that tempt you to think of this world as home?

- Even with all the truly good things in this life, why is it dangerous to get too cozy down here?

- What are the possible risks of living as a child of Heaven?

Why are they worthwhile?

• What's one new way you need to plug into God's family, your home away from Home?

• What is something on earth that your Father might be asking you to let go of, in order to stand up for him?

When my father learned that I was a Christian, he told me to choose God or him. I chose the Lord because I have understood that He is the only thing really worthy for me.[2]
—Rosa's letter from Cuba
Day 7, PRAY21 DISCOVERY GUIDE

SECURE CHANNEL

Here's space for you to "pray on paper," writing out your conversation with God about living on earth with a view to your heavenly Home.

Prayer for myself:

Prayer for my partners (or others):

LOOSE ENDS

As you were reading, thinking, and praying today, did any questions come to mind that were left unanswered? Write them here, so you can ask your partners or research them later on your own.

One-Week Checkpoint

Time to stop and take stock of what you've learned so far. Is God's dream for your life becoming a little more clear? You can answer these questions on your own or with others, but it's especially important to share your specific commitment (Questions 5 and 6) with your partners, so you can support and encourage each other.

1. During the last seven days, what has been the most encouraging, uplifting thought you've had working through this *Discovery Guide*?

    _____

    _____

    _____

    _____

2. What has been the hardest idea or challenge for you to swallow?

    _____

    _____

    _____

    _____ Why do you think this is so hard for you?

    _____

    _____

    _____

3. How have others been helpful to you as you've sought to learn and grow? What more could the rest of us do for you?

    _____

    _____

    _____

    _____

4. Have you been able to pray for, encourage, or lovingly challenge one or more of your partners toward growth? If so, describe one way you've done this.

5. Look back over your journaling for these first seven days. Think about the talks you've had with your partners. Does one challenge stand out as God's next step of growth and obedience for you? What is it?

6. **Rubber Meets the Road:** Write down a few details for following through on that next step. For example, what exactly will you do? When? Where? With whom? Who will support you and hold you accountable? How will you know when you've fulfilled your commitment? (Hint: Make your goal stretching and a little risky, but not unrealistic, so you don't just give up.)

7. From these first seven days, what other growth areas, goals, or commitments would you like to pursue some day? Write down a few of those dreams. You can come back to them later.

what's easier to fix—
body or heart?

Oh, what joy for those whose disobedience is forgiven, whose sin is put out of sight! Yes, what joy for those whose record the LORD has cleared of guilt, whose lives are lived in complete honesty!

PSALM 32:1–2, NLT

The Spirit of God, the Master, is on me because God anointed me.
He sent me to preach good news to the poor, heal the heartbroken,
Announce freedom to all captives, pardon all prisoners.
God sent me to announce the year of his grace—a celebration of God's
*   destruction of our enemies—and to comfort all who mourn,*
To care for the needs of all who mourn in Zion, give them bouquets of
*   roses instead of ashes,*
Messages of joy instead of news of doom, a praising heart instead of a
*   languid spirit.*

ISAIAH 61:1–3

I was given the gift of a handicap to keep me in constant touch with my limitations.... At first I didn't think of it as a gift, and begged God to remove it. Three times I did that, and then he told me, "My grace is enough; it's all you need. My strength comes into its own in your weakness."

2 CORINTHIANS 12:7–9

God is a Healer, and he cares about every kind of injury or illness. He's capable of healing any of them, but he's especially concerned about your spiritual injuries—sin—which stand between you and him. These he promises to heal and cleanse absolutely when you ask him to. You can trust that his forgiveness makes you totally acceptable to him.

BRIEF DEBRIEF

When we hurt or feel dirty, it can be hard to believe God cares. He does. Try to hang onto his compassion as you work through these questions, whether on your own or with your partners.

• Do you have trouble believing in God's complete forgiveness and acceptance of you? Can you explain why?

If he's forgiven you, have you forgiven your-self, or sought forgiveness from others? How might these bring you freedom?

• Is some physical or emotional injury keeping you stuck? If so, explain why. (See also Day 14.)

• Consider your fitness for God's mission. What one specific
  healing (of sin, emotions, or body) would you request?

• Once you've prayed for this, how can you step out in faith that the Healer
  has granted it, will grant it over time, or will enable you to live well even
  with this injury?

When I became a Christian, all my
friends told me, "Come as you are
and God will change you, but don't
think you have to change to come to
God." I came with all my baggage.³
                    —Billy Buchanan's story
          Day 8, PRAY21 DISCOVERY GUIDE

S ᴇᴄᴜʀᴇ C ʜᴀɴɴᴇʟ

After you've recorded your conversation with God about your requests for healing, consider putting a reminder on your calendar a few months down the road. Check back to see how he's responded to your prayers.

Prayer for myself:

_____

_____

_____

_____

_____

_____

Prayer for my partners (or others):

_____

_____

_____

_____

_____

L ᴏᴏꜱᴇ E ɴᴅꜱ

As you were reading, thinking, and praying today, did any questions come to mind that were left unanswered? Write them here, so you can ask your partners or research them later on your own.

who loves God more?

Levi held a banquet in his home with Jesus as the guest of honor. Many of Levi's fellow tax collectors and other guests also ate with them. But the Pharisees and their teachers of religious law complained bitterly to Jesus' disciples, "Why do you eat and drink with such scum?"

Jesus answered them, "Healthy people don't need a doctor—sick people do. I have come to call not those who think they are righteous, but those who know they are sinners and need to repent."

LUKE 5:29–32, NLT

I'm so grateful to Christ Jesus for making me [Paul] adequate to do this work. He went out on a limb, you know, in trusting me with this ministry. The only credentials I brought to it were invective and witch hunts and arrogance. But I was treated mercifully because I didn't know what I was doing—didn't know Who I was doing it against! Grace mixed with faith and love poured over me and into me. And all because of Jesus.

Here's a word you can take to heart and depend on: Jesus Christ came into the world to save sinners. I'm proof—Public Sinner Number One—of someone who could never have made it apart from sheer mercy. And now he shows me off—evidence of his endless patience—to those who are right on the edge of trusting him forever.

1 TIMOTHY 1:12–16

We become trapped by labels that we place on ourselves or accept from others. But no matter what you've done or become, Jesus dismisses the labels when you become his. You can dismiss them, too.

BRIEF DEBRIEF

Labels are sticky. Use the following questions to identify yours, and ask God to help you give them to him, as often as it takes to lose them completely. Let your partners help with this.

• What labels do others put on you?

Which labels are you most likely to let stick?

• Why do you believe them?

A label on a can of food informs you. A label on a person enslaves you.

—Day 9, PRAY21 DISCOVERY GUIDE

• Is there a difference between a sinful pattern of living and a label? If so, what's the difference?

How do their solutions differ?

• If you haven't invited Jesus to forgive your sins, why not now? If you have, but you're still attached to an old label, how can you become convinced the label's a lie? (Truth: You're completely acceptable to your Father.)

What's your first step?

SECURE CHANNEL

By writing out your prayers about your and others' labels, you're recording a moment of clarity that you might need to revisit later, when things get foggy again.

Prayer for myself: _____

_____

_____

_____

_____

_____

Prayer for my partners (or others): _____

_____

_____

_____

_____

_____

 # LOOSE ENDS

As you were reading, thinking, and praying today, did any questions come to mind that were left unanswered? Write them here, so you can ask your partners or research them later on your own.

what are you after?

In the beginning the Word already existed. The Word was with God, and the Word was God.... The Word became human and made his home among us. He was full of unfailing love and faithfulness. And we have seen his glory, the glory of the Father's one and only Son.

JOHN 1:1, 14, NLT

The Word of Life appeared right before our eyes; we saw it happen! And now we're telling you in most sober prose that what we witnessed was, incredibly, this: The infinite Life of God himself took shape before us.

We saw it, we heard it, and now we're telling you so you can experience it along with us, this experience of communion with the Father and his Son, Jesus Christ. Our motive for writing is simply this: We want you to enjoy this, too. Your joy will double our joy!

1 JOHN 1:2–4

The members of the council were amazed when they saw the boldness of Peter and John, for they could see that they were ordinary men with no special training in the Scriptures. They also recognized them as men who had been with Jesus.

ACTS 4:13, NLT

Knowing Jesus in the flesh was a special privilege for his first disciples. But we now have the greater privilege of having him live *within* us, all the time. Take full advantage of this astounding friendship!

BRIEF DEBRIEF

Remind yourself often of Jesus' Presence with you, in you, all around you, while you wrestle with these questions, whether on your own or with your partners.

- Have you ever wished you could have been with Jesus in the flesh? How would that have been better?

- What's better about the kind of relationship you can have with him now?

Today, how deep can a person's friendship with Christ go?

- What do you do to spend time with Jesus?

Does it help you understand him better,

or allow you to be more open to him?

• What's something new or something more that you want to do to
deepen your friendship with him?

What's your first step?

Hanging out with Jesus was
refreshing, challenging, enlivening,
clarifying... Indefinably normal.
Frightening in a fascinating way.
—Andrew's story
Day 10, PRAY21 DISCOVERY GUIDE

SECURE CHANNEL

Write your thoughts and prayers here as you bathe in Jesus' Presence today. Let this be one of many conversations with him. Let them be often and long.

Prayer for myself:

_____

_____

_____

_____

_____

_____

_____

Prayer for my partners (or others):

_____

_____

_____

_____

_____

_____

LOOSE ENDS

As you were reading, thinking, and praying today, did any questions come to mind that were left unanswered? Write them here, so you can ask your partners or research them later on your own.

are you
really listening?

The heavens proclaim the glory of God. The skies display his craftsmanship. Day after day they continue to speak; night after night they make him known. They speak without a sound or word; their voice is never heard. Yet their message has gone throughout the earth, and their words to all the world.

PSALM 19:1–4, NLT

You must all be quick to listen, slow to speak, and slow to get angry.... Don't just listen to God's word. You must do what it says. Otherwise, you are only fooling yourselves. For if you listen to the word and don't obey, it is like glancing at your face in a mirror. You see yourself, walk away, and forget what you look like. But if you look carefully into the perfect law that sets you free, and if you do what it says and don't forget what you heard, then God will bless you for doing it.

JAMES 1:19, 22–25, NLT

The Lord was with Samuel as he grew up, and he let none of his words fall to the ground.

1 SAMUEL 3:19, NIV

Jesus is speaking all the time, especially to his true followers, in whom he lives. It pays to listen. Really listen. And that means accepting even the hard stuff—his truth is good medicine. Let it change you inside...and outwardly in your living.

BRIEF DEBRIEF

Listening is two-way. By writing your thoughts, you allow God to respond and guide your thinking in good directions. With your partners, talk and listen out loud about these questions.

• How well have you been listening to God lately?

What makes listening hard for you?

• Describe one time you listened well, or a time you wish you had listened better. What happened?

• How can you tell the difference between truth
  from God—through any avenue of communication—
  and something that's not his truth?

• What is one thing you think God is trying to tell you now?

• How, specifically, will you show him in
  word and action that you're really listening?

Such a big difference between
"Why didn't I listen?" and "At
your service, Lord."

—Day 11, PRAY21 DISCOVERY GUIDE

SECURE CHANNEL

What do you want to tell God? He's listening. What is he saying to you?

Prayer for myself: _____

_____

_____

_____

_____

_____

_____

Prayer for my partners (or others): _____

_____

_____

_____

_____

_____

LOOSE ENDS

As you were reading, thinking, and praying today, did any questions come to mind that were left unanswered? Write them here, so you can ask your partners or research them later on your own.

who do
you say I am?

"If a person climbs over or through the fence of a sheep pen instead of going through the gate, you know he's up to no good—a sheep rustler! The shepherd walks right up to the gate.... The sheep recognize his voice. He calls his own sheep by name and leads them out. When he gets them all out, he leads them and they follow because they are familiar with his voice. They won't follow a stranger's voice but will scatter because they aren't used to the sound of it.

"I [Jesus] am the Gate for the sheep. All those others are up to no good—sheep stealers, every one of them. But the sheep didn't listen to them. I am the Gate. Anyone who goes through me will be cared for—will freely go in and out, and find pasture. A thief is only there to steal and kill and destroy. I came so they can have real and eternal life, more and better life than they ever dreamed of.

"I am the Good Shepherd. The Good Shepherd puts the sheep before himself, sacrifices himself if necessary. A hired man is not a real shepherd. The sheep mean nothing to him. He sees a wolf come and runs for it, leaving the sheep to be ravaged and scattered by the wolf. He's only in it for the money. The sheep don't matter to him.

"I am the Good Shepherd. I know my own sheep and my own sheep know me.... I put the sheep before myself, sacrificing myself if necessary."

JOHN 10:1–5, 7–15

Dear friends, do not believe everyone who claims to speak by the Spirit. You must test them to see if the spirit they have comes from God. For there are many false prophets in the world.... If someone claims to be a prophet and does not acknowledge the truth about Jesus, that person is not from God. Such a person has the spirit of the Antichrist.... You belong to God, my dear children. You have already won a victory over those people, because the Spirit who lives in you is greater than the spirit who lives in the world.

1 JOHN 4:1, 3–4, NLT

The world is full of counterfeit christs. If you really want to see the genuine Jesus, he'll show himself to you, and there'll be no mistaking him for one of the imposters. Seek him. Let him be who he really is, not who you wish he was.

BRIEF DEBRIEF

As you dig deep into these questions, think of your written notes as a verbal "Wanted" poster—clarifying the counterfeits you want to banish, as well as the true Lord you want as your permanent roommate.

• Describe the false jesus who most easily fools you when you let your guard down.

• How is the real Christ different and better?

- Who do you say Jesus is? Choose an answer that zeroes in on the Truth[4] and clearly sets him off from the fakes. Your answer can be as long or short as you need.

- Name one visible difference your Lord will make in your life this week.

Secure Channel

Talk with God on paper about your desire and efforts to zero in on the authentic Jesus. Ask him to show himself genuine by making a difference in the way you live.

Prayer for myself:

_____

_____

_____

_____

_____

_____

_____

Prayer for my partners (or others):

_____

_____

_____

_____

_____

_____

Loose Ends

As you were reading, thinking, and praying today, did any questions come to mind that were left unanswered? Write them here, so you can ask your partners or research them later on your own.

who doesn't first figure the cost?

Why are you so polite with me [Jesus], always saying "Yes, sir," and "That's right, sir," but never doing a thing I tell you? These words I speak to you are not mere additions to your life, homeowner improvements to your standard of living. They are foundation words, words to build a life on. If you work the words into your life, you are like a smart carpenter who dug deep and laid the foundation of his house on bedrock. When the river burst its banks and crashed against the house, nothing could shake it; it was built to last. But if you just use my words in Bible studies and don't work them into your life, you are like a dumb carpenter who built a house but skipped the foundation. When the swollen river came crashing in, it collapsed like a house of cards. It was a total loss.

LUKE 6:46–49

Look, I [Jesus] am sending you out as sheep among wolves. So be as shrewd as snakes and harmless as doves. But beware! For you will be handed over to the courts and will be flogged with whips in the synagogues. You will stand trial before governors and kings because you are my followers. But this will be your opportunity to tell the rulers and other unbelievers about me. When you are arrested, don't worry about how to respond or what to say. God will give you the right words at the right time. For it is not you who will be speaking—it will be the Spirit of your Father speaking through you.

MATTHEW 10:16–20, NLT

Don't be bluffed into silence by the threats of bullies. There's nothing they can do to your soul, your core being. Save your fear for God, who holds your entire life—body and soul—in his hands.

MATTHEW 10:28

Talk, but no walk? That's not a disciple. "Gain" without ever any pain? Not a disciple. Squeaking by with minimum investment of self? No dice.

Hand it all over to Jesus—everything you are, everything you have. *That's* a disciple. Once you've done it, you'll never want to live any other way.

B R I E F   D E B R I E F

Yesterday you wrote a verbal "Wanted" poster. Today you're filling out a balance sheet. Cost versus return. When the "cost" column adds up to 100 percent, the "return" column is going to need a lot more paper.

• What, if anything, keeps you from selling out to God? Something "better"? Fear of pain or loss? Be specific.

• Brainstorm several benefits of living for God. Consider how much each of them really means.

• Selling out is risky. How does God promise to reimburse, protect, and strengthen you?

• Write your gift list to God. What does "everything" include in your life?

• How you will go about giving him his first gift from your list?

"What does your life amount to if you're not adding to the kingdom of the Lord? Make your life count for something bigger than yourself."

—Josh Weidmann quote
Day 13, PRAY21 DISCOVERY GUIDE

Secure Channel

The prayers you write here can be a tentative market inquiry, a hopeful letter of intent, or a confirmed deed of sale. Jesus calls you to sell out completely to him, but he leaves the point of decision up to you.

Prayer for myself:

Prayer for my partners (or others):

 ### Loose Ends

As you were reading, thinking, and praying today, did any questions come to mind that were left unanswered? Write them here, so you can ask your partners or research them later on your own.

do you want to get well?

Jesus said, "Come to me, all of you who are weary and carry heavy burdens, and I will give you rest. Take my yoke upon you. Let me teach you, because I am humble and gentle at heart, and you will find rest for your souls. For my yoke is easy to bear, and the burden I give you is light."

MATTHEW 11:28–30, NLT

Get along among yourselves, each of you doing your part. Our counsel is that you warn the freeloaders to get a move on. Gently encourage the stragglers, and reach out for the exhausted, pulling them to their feet. Be patient with each person, attentive to individual needs. And be careful that when you get on each other's nerves you don't snap at each other. Look for the best in each other, and always do your best to bring it out.

1 THESSALONIANS 5:13–15

This is the crisis we're in: God-light streamed into the world, but men and women everywhere ran for the darkness. They went for the darkness because they were not really interested in pleasing God. Everyone who makes a practice of doing evil, addicted to denial and illusion, hates God-light and won't come near it, fearing a painful exposure. But anyone working and living in truth and reality welcomes God-light so the work can be seen for the God-work it is.

JOHN 3:19–21

We've all be wounded in life. Spiritually, emotionally, physically. At our own hand, by others, and by life's impersonal accidents. God offers healing… restoration to the fully functioning Christ-follower you were always meant to be. But healing sometimes means frightening change, hard work, and pain. It's okay to be afraid, but go ahead…put yourself in the Doctor's care. You can trust him.

BRIEF DEBRIEF

Work through the following self-diagnosis with God's help, and with the help of your partners. If you'll be honest, and follow Doctor's orders, full recovery in heart is guaranteed.

• A huge number of people, young and old, have emotional and spiritual illnesses and wounds inside. Pain from abuse, rejection, or neglect. Horrible self-image. Destructive habits and addictions. Depression… A lot of people prefer to stay sick. Why? What good do they think they're getting out of their condition?

• Do you know someone who doesn't want to get well? Don't mention names.

How might Jesus try talking them into accepting his healing?

My "helplessness" was sin. God wanted me to depend on him...and do some-thing. I did nothing. I robbed him.
—The crippled man's story
Day 14, PRAY21 DISCOVERY GUIDE

- How about you? Are you resisting
  God's healing in some way?

  Do you know why?

- How might your life be different
  if you let him make you well?

- What specific steps would lead to your healing? (Consider, for example,
  prayer, confession, accountability, learning God's truth, getting counsel-
  ing or rehab.)

  What do you want to do first?

Secure Channel

If you're willing, your prayer here will be your pledge to accept God's healing and, along with it, the grown-up responsibility of the healthy. If you're not ready, talk with God about the reasons. He'll work with you.

Prayer for myself:

Prayer for my partners (or others):

Loose Ends

As you were reading, thinking, and praying today, did any questions come to mind that were left unanswered? Write them here, so you can ask your partners or research them later on your own.

Two-Week Checkpoint

Time once again to consolidate your spiritual gains. Hopefully, you're being challenged in a way that might be scary, but you're also being encouraged by God's wisdom, power, and love. He's big enough.

Whether you work through these questions alone or with your partners, be sure to tell them your specific commitment for this week (Questions 5 and 6). You need them beside you, asking hard questions, praying, convincing you that you can do it.

1. How are you feeling at this stage? Tired? Pumped? Scared? Important? Something else? Do you know why?

2. In one or two sentences, how are you now seeing the bigger picture of God's mission for his people on earth?

3. In one or two sentences, summarize your current understanding of God's call for you as a specialist-on-assignment in that mission.

4. How have your partners been helpful to you this week? How have you helped them? ....

....

....

5. Review all you've read, considered, and discussed during this second week (Days 8–14). What is the one new step of growth and obedience you think God wants you to take? It might be brand new for you, or it might be raising the bar on an existing goal. (It might even be one of your "leftover" dream goals from Question 7, One-Week Checkpoint.)

....

....

....

....

6. **Rubber Meets the Road:** Write down the necessary particulars that you need for true follow-through on your commitment. Be sure to include a plan for support and accountability from others. And be sure you have a way of determining whether you're accomplishing your goal. Take a real risk, but keep your commitment real (within your reach to achieve).

....

....

....

....

7. From Days 8–14, what other growth areas, goals, or commitments would you like to pursue some day? Write them down as reminders for later.

....

....

....

should I beg
for escape?

I want to drink God, deep draughts of God.

I'm thirsty for God-alive. I wonder, "Will I ever make it—arrive and drink in God's presence?"

I'm on a diet of tears—tears for breakfast, tears for supper....

Why are you down in the dumps, dear soul? Why are you crying the blues?

Fix my eyes on God—soon I'll be praising again.

He puts a smile on my face. He's my God....

Chaos calls to chaos, to the tune of whitewater rapids. Your breaking surf, your thundering breakers crash and crush me.

Then God promises to love me all day, sing songs all through the night! My life is God's prayer.

Sometimes I ask God, my rock-solid God, "Why did you let me down?"...

Why are you down in the dumps, dear soul? Why are you crying the blues?

Fix my eyes on God—soon I'll be praising again.

He puts a smile on my face. He's my God....

I counted on you, God. Why did you walk out on me? Why am I pacing the floor, wringing my hands...?

Give me your lantern and compass, give me a map, so I can find my way to the sacred mountain, to the place of your presence,

To enter the place of worship, meet my exuberant God, sing my thanks with a harp, magnificent God, my God.

Why are you down in the dumps, dear soul? Why are you crying the blues?

Fix my eyes on God—soon I'll be praising again.

He puts a smile on my face. He's my God.

PSALMS 42:1–3, 5, 7–9, 11; 43:2–5

When life knocks you down, take God's sympathetic hand and let him help you up. When you can't get up, he lies down and hurts with you; feel his comfort. And when you think your nightmare is eternal, scream to God and hang onto him; he'll bring morning light in time.

B R I E F   D E B R I E F

If life is smooth sailing right now, your responses to these questions can be part of your emergency preparations. If life is a hurricane at the moment, follow this beacon to the lifeline. Be sure to let your partners in on your experiences and thoughts.

• Describe a time when you've wished desperately that God, or someone, would rescue you from your pain. (Maybe right now.)

How can both honesty about your pain and genuine faith in God work together in those times?

• How long did it take you to heal, if you ever did?

What helped?

What didn't?

• No one can escape fear and grief when enduring a loss. But brainstorm some ways you can prepare during the easier seasons of life, so you'll hang onto both God and hope when you have to ride out the hard times.

• What's the one step you will take this week to prepare for a future crisis, or to make it through one right now?

She told God how much she hurt. And even though she didn't have any clue about the whys, she knew the Who. She said, "I trust you."

—Tammy Trent's story

Day 15, PRAY21 DISCOVERY GUIDE

SECURE CHANNEL

Whether your hardest times are past, present, or future, talk about them with your Father, who is timelessly present with you.

Prayer for myself:

Prayer for my partners (or others):

LOOSE ENDS

As you were reading, thinking, and praying today, did any questions come to mind that were left unanswered? Write them here, so you can ask your partners or research them later on your own.

didn't you know I had to be about my Father's business?

The servant who [was entrusted by his master with] five bags of silver began to invest the money and earned five more.... After a long time their master returned from his trip and called them to give an account of how they had used his money. The servant to whom he had entrusted the five bags of silver came forward with five more and said, "Master, you gave me five bags of silver to invest, and I have earned five more."

The master was full of praise. "Well done, my good and faithful servant. You have been faithful in handling this small amount, so now I will give you many more responsibilities. Let's celebrate together!"

MATTHEW 25:16, 19–21, NLT

You...must be ready all the time, for the Son of Man will come when least expected. A faithful, sensible servant is one to whom the master can give the responsibility of managing his other household servants and feeding them. If the master returns and finds that the servant has done a good job, there will be a reward. I tell you the truth, the master will put that servant in charge of all he owns.

MATTHEW 24:44–47, NLT

———

Whatever your age, your heavenly Father has important work for you to do—kingdom work. Take him seriously. Take yourself seriously. Follow Jesus' example and show yourself to be a faithful, reliable child of your Father.

BRIEF DEBRIEF

Write your thoughts, and your Father's thoughts, about the eternally important earth-business he's assigning you. Be sure to interact with your partners about it.

- What are the traditional boundaries limiting the ways "kids" can serve in church?

Which of these do you think are biblical boundaries?

Which might not be?

- Can you describe one time that you or someone you know served God in an unexpected way—unexpected, maybe, because of age, abilities, personality, background, or some other pigeonhole?

Jesus trembled. "You'll guide me, right, Father?"
    Absolutely. You'll do fine, Son. I love you. I'm so proud of you.   —Young Jesus' story
    Day 16, PRAY21 DISCOVERY GUIDE

- What is your Father's business?

- How does he want you
  to be doing it in church?

  Outside church?

- What's one significant new step you
  want to take to serve your Father?

Secure Channel

In order to do God's work and do it well, you need to keep in close contact with him, for guidance, strength, and passion.

Prayer for myself: _____

_____

_____

_____

_____

_____

_____

Prayer for my partners (or others): _____

_____

_____

_____

_____

_____

 ## Loose Ends

As you were reading, thinking, and praying today, did any questions come to mind that were left unanswered? Write them here, so you can ask your partners or research them later on your own.

won't God answer his children's persistent prayers?

Keep on asking, and you will receive what you ask for. Keep on seeking, and you will find. Keep on knocking, and the door will be opened to you. For everyone who asks, receives. Everyone who seeks, finds. And to everyone who knocks, the door will be opened.

LUKE 11:9–10, NLT

Prayer is essential in this ongoing warfare [against the Devil and his demons]. Pray hard and long. Pray for your brothers and sisters. Keep your eyes open. Keep each other's spirits up so that no one falls behind or drops out.

EPHESIANS 6:18

Don't fret or worry. Instead of worrying, pray. Let petitions and praises shape your worries into prayers, letting God know your concerns. Before you know it, a sense of God's wholeness, everything coming together for good, will come and settle you down. It's wonderful what happens when Christ displaces worry at the center of your life.

PHILIPPIANS 4:6–7

Pray all the time; thank God no matter what happens. This is the way God wants you who belong to Christ Jesus to live.

1 THESSALONIANS 5:17–18

Praying to an invisible Father, it's sometimes hard to believe that he's there, that he cares, and that he listens. Especially when you don't get any response for a long time. But take him at his word. He's there, he cares, he listens, and he will answer your prayer in the very best way and the very best timing. Keep praying.

BRIEF DEBRIEF

Test the phone line between you and God. It's not broken at his end. If it needs repair at your end, invite him to help. And make it a team effort with your partners.

• When you pray, do you think God is listening? _____
  Do you think he cares about your requests? _____

  _____

  _____

  _____

  _____

                                                    Why or why not?

  _____

  _____

  _____

• There are a variety of ways to communicate with God. Take a minute and brainstorm creatively about ways that might work best for you. (Think about all the ways people communicate—speaking, writing, body language, art, music, actions, and more. How might you use these for relating to God?)

  _____

  _____

  _____

  _____

  _____

  _____

  _____

• What are a couple of God-honoring

  desires you want more than anything else?

• What is your strategy for bringing

  these requests regularly to God?

What is your first step?

He now knew that twenty-two years
of prayer had been worth every
second. Both of his parents would
be waiting for him in heaven.

—Randy Alcorn's story
Day 17, PRAY21 DISCOVERY GUIDE

SECURE CHANNEL

Praying about prayer? Why not? In whatever words come to you, talk to God about persistence and creativity in your prayer life. And anything else you want to bring up.

Prayer for myself:

Prayer for my partners (or others):

LOOSE ENDS

As you were reading, thinking, and praying today, did any questions come to mind that were left unanswered? Write them here, so you can ask your partners or research them later on your own.

DAY 18

do you put a lamp under the bed?

Let your good deeds shine out for all to see, so that everyone will praise your heavenly Father.

MATTHEW 5:16, NLT

Do you see how this story works?... The farmer plants the Word. Some people are like the seed that falls on the hardened soil of the road. No sooner do they hear the Word than Satan snatches away what has been planted in them. And some are like the seed that lands in the gravel. When they first hear the Word, they respond with great enthusiasm. But there is such shallow soil of character that when the emotions wear off and some difficulty arrives, there is nothing to show for it. The seed cast in the weeds represents the ones who hear the kingdom news but are overwhelmed with worries about all the things they have to do and all the things they want to get. The stress strangles what they heard, and nothing comes of it. But the seed planted in the good earth represents those who hear the Word, embrace it, and produce a harvest beyond their wildest dreams.

MARK 4:13–20

God wants everyone on earth to know him. You're his spotlight, pointing to him, making his heart obvious, unveiling his truth for the world. Shine!

You're also his seed of life, planted on earth. By dying to self, you can take the life he's given you and multiply it hundreds and thousands of times in other people.

BRIEF DEBRIEF

Wrestle with these questions. Whether you do this on your own or with your partners, be sure at some time to share your key thoughts and commitments with them. Ask them to help you shine.

- Think about your life on earth so far. What will you be remembered for when you're gone? What will people say at your funeral?

- What have you contributed to the lives of those around you?

How are they different because you lived?

• What's one simple but stretching step you will take this week to shine God's love and truth into the lives of others?

• What has to die in order for this to happen?

• What support or resources do you need from others this week?

What do they need from you?

Rachael chose to hold high her
10,000-watt halogen, visible to
all, as she walked the halls of her
school. And people saw Jesus.[5]
—Rachael's story
Day 18, PRAY21 DISCOVERY GUIDE

Secure Channel

You have two related topics to hash over with God—shining...and dying. Both can be scary. But both lead to eternal life in others, and more abundant life for you.

Prayer for myself:

_____

_____

_____

_____

_____

_____

Prayer for my partners (or others):

_____

_____

_____

_____

_____

 ## Loose Ends

As you were reading, thinking, and praying today, did any questions come to mind that were left unanswered? Write them here, so you can ask your partners or research them later on your own.

do you really
love me?

Love your enemies. Let them bring out the best in you, not the worst. When someone gives you a hard time, respond with the energies of prayer for that person. If someone slaps you in the face, stand there and take it. If someone grabs your shirt, giftwrap your best coat and make a present of it. If someone takes unfair advantage of you, use the occasion to practice the servant life. No more tit-for-tat stuff. Live generously.

Here is a simple rule of thumb for behavior: Ask yourself what you want people to do for you; then grab the initiative and do it for them! If you only love the lovable, do you expect a pat on the back? Run-of-the-mill sinners do that. If you only help those who help you, do you expect a medal? Garden-variety sinners do that. If you only give for what you hope to get out of it, do you think that's charity? The stingiest of pawnbrokers does that.

I tell you, love your enemies. Help and give without expecting a return. You'll never—I promise—regret it. Live out this God-created identity the way our Father lives toward us, generously and graciously, even when we're at our worst. Our Father is kind; you be kind.

Don't pick on people, jump on their failures, criticize their faults—unless, of course, you want the same treatment. Don't condemn those who are down; that hardness can boomerang. Be easy on people; you'll find life a lot easier. Give away your life; you'll find life given back, but not merely given back—given back with bonus and blessing. Giving, not getting, is the way. Generosity begets generosity.

LUKE 6:27–38

You love Jesus? Great. That means you love people, too. Even the hard-to-love ones. Because Jesus said the way to love him is to love them.

BRIEF DEBRIEF

Write your thoughts honestly—even the ones you're not
proud of. Your openness with God and with trustworthy
people is the best way to change the things you don't like in yourself.

• What kind of people do you have the hardest time loving?

Why do you think this is?

• Talk about God's attitude toward those same people.
Try to get inside his heart and see through his eyes.
Try to imagine how he honestly feels toward them.

"If you love me, take care of
those I love—all of them. And not
just with a prayer and a smile,
but with your life. That's how you
really love me."
—Paraphrase of Jesus
Day 19, PRAY21 DISCOVERY GUIDE

Does it help your attitude?

• What is one opportunity in your daily life to do something kind for an "unlovable" person?

• The mere doing is good and loving, but how can you cultivate a heart that honestly wants to?

What's your first step?

Secure Channel

You need Jesus to help you love Jesus, because you need help loving people. So—for the love of Jesus—ask him for help.

Prayer for myself:

Prayer for my partners (or others):

 ## Loose Ends

As you were reading, thinking, and praying today, did any questions come to mind that were left unanswered? Write them here, so you can ask your partners or research them later on your own.

are you able to drink from the same cup as me?

I [Paul] want you to know...that everything that has happened to me here has helped to spread the Good News. For everyone here, including the whole palace guard, knows that I am in chains because of Christ. And because of my imprisonment, most of the believers here have gained confidence and boldly speak God's message without fear.... I trust that my life will bring honor to Christ, whether I live or die. For to me, living means living for Christ, and dying is even better.

PHILIPPIANS 1:12–14, 20–21, NLT

Don't push your way to the front; don't sweet-talk your way to the top. Put yourself aside, and help others get ahead. Don't be obsessed with getting your own advantage. Forget yourselves long enough to lend a helping hand.

Think of yourselves the way Christ Jesus thought of himself. He had equal status with God but didn't think so much of himself that he had to cling to the advantages of that status no matter what. Not at all. When the time came, he set aside the privileges of deity and took on the status of a slave, became human! Having become human, he stayed human. It was an incredibly humbling process. He didn't claim special privileges. Instead, he lived a selfless, obedient life and then died a selfless, obedient death—and the worst kind of death at that—a crucifixion. Because of that obedience, God lifted him high and honored him far beyond anyone or anything, ever.

PHILIPPIANS 2:3–9

The privilege of being Jesus' disciple goes hand in hand with some responsibilities. Following Jesus means eventually following him all the way to glorious eternity. But between here and there lies the way of the cross. Frightening? Yes. Doable? You bet, with God's help. Worthwhile? Well, let's put it this way: You're not even a disciple if you don't carry your cross.[6]

BRIEF DEBRIEF

Not all pain is bad. And not all humiliation is bad. As we follow and serve Jesus, he calls us all to both at one time or another. Use these questions— with your partners or on your own—to adjust your expectations about life as a disciple.

• Jesus asks you the question he asked James and John: "Are you able to drink the same cup I drank?" What's your honest answer at this moment?

If you're not happy with that answer, what might help you change it?

- Jesus might some day ask you to suffer physically for him. But what are other ways he's likely to ask you to serve and suffer for him?

- What step of service or sacrifice is he asking you to take now?

How will you start?

Secure Channel

Here's space for you to "pray on paper," writing out your conversation with God about serving and suffering in the name of Christ.

Prayer for myself:

_____
_____
_____
_____
_____
_____
_____

Prayer for my partners (or others):

_____
_____
_____
_____
_____
_____

 ## Loose Ends

As you were reading, thinking, and praying today, did any questions come to mind that were left unanswered? Write them here, so you can ask your partners or research them later on your own.

will you really die for me?

"Come now, let us reason together," says the Lord. "Though your sins are like scarlet, they shall be as white as snow; though they are red as crimson, they shall be like wool."

ISAIAH 1:18, NIV

[Jesus] used his servant body to carry our sins to the Cross so we could be rid of sin, free to live the right way. His wounds became your healing. You were lost sheep with no idea who you were or where you were going. Now you're named and kept for good by the Shepherd of your souls.

1 PETER 2:24–25

Since Christ suffered physical pain, you must arm yourselves with the same attitude he had, and be ready to suffer, too. For if you have suffered physically for Christ, you have finished with sin. You won't spend the rest of your lives chasing your own desires, but you will be anxious to do the will of God.

1 PETER 4:1–2, NLT

All of you, serve each other in humility, for "God opposes the proud but favors the humble." So humble yourselves under the mighty power of God, and at the right time he will lift you up in honor.

1 PETER 5:5–6, NLT

What do you do when you've failed Jesus? When you've let him down in a *huge* way? You might be sad and sorry for a while—that's okay. But don't just stay isolated in perpetual mourning. That doesn't do Jesus any good. Let him forgive you, help you back up, and get you back in action. He wants to fix your friendship with him, and he wants you serving his kingdom.

Brief Debrief

These questions should help you take sin and failure very seriously. But they should help you take forgiveness and restoration seriously, too. Hang onto both sides of this balance. Sin is bad. Forgiveness is complete.

• How big a deal does the idea of failing Jesus seem to you?

Explain your answer.

• What does Jesus honestly think and feel about the times you fail him?

- What's the way of dealing with your failures that makes Jesus happiest?

- Can you think of a past or present failure that still has you down, out of God's game?

- How will you confront that failure, and get back on with the mission?

I knew Jesus was saying, "That's right, Peter, you hurt me bad. But I didn't give up on you. So don't give up on yourself. You're forgiven. I want you on my crew." —Peter's story

Day 21, PRAY21 DISCOVERY GUIDE

SECURE CHANNEL

Record your thoughts here as you talk with God—alone and with your partners—about recovery from your failures.

Prayer for myself: _____

_____

_____

_____

_____

_____

_____

Prayer for my partners (or others): _____

_____

_____

_____

_____

_____

LOOSE ENDS

As you were reading, thinking, and praying today, did any questions come to mind that were left unanswered? Write them here, so you can ask your partners or research them later on your own.

Three-Week Checkpoint

As you wrap up your 21-day venture, stop and bring it all into focus. It's time to settle on your third key commitment. Be sure to share this specific commitment (Questions 3–5) with your partners, making them part of its fulfillment.

Plan together how Pray21 will become Pray365, beginning by simply keeping in touch for the next couple of months. Sharing frustrations, breakthroughs, mess-ups, and victories. Asking each other the hard questions. *Being* God's kingdom mission team together.

1. As best you can right now, finish this sentence: *I think the mission to which God is calling me is…* (Stay open to mission clarification or reassignment later.)

2. What is one specific ministry opportunity you want to pursue as part of this mission? Something you're already doing, or something new? Something boldly visible, or making a difference behind the scenes? Pouring all of yourself into one activity, or touching several causes, each in a significant way? Don't be afraid to dream.

3. From the topics and challenges of this third week (Days 15–21), choose your third new step of growth and obedience. It could be something new, or turning up the dial on a goal you've already been pursuing. Or

it might come from your "leftover" dream goals listed under Question 7 in the One-Week or the Two-Week Checkpoints. _____

_____

_____

_____

4. **Rubber Meets the Road:** Write down your specific plan for follow-through. Will this commitment stretch you? Is it reachable for you? How will you measure success for this goal? _____

_____

_____

_____

_____

5. **Rubber Meets the Road:** Take out your schedules, PDAs, Blackberries… or even just that napkin over there. Set specific dates, times, and places for at least eight weekly progress check-ins with each other. Meeting in person is best, but phone is good. _____

_____

_____

_____

_____

6. Write down any other growth areas or commitments from Days 15–21 that you would like to pursue some day. (Idea: Put reminders to yourself in your schedule to look back at these ideas once each month. Regularly reevaluate your current goals, and adjust as needed.) _____

_____

_____

_____

_____

Endnotes

1 The language in this quote is slightly updated to contemporary English.

2 From "Sowing God's Word" in *Jesus Freaks Vol II*, by dc Talk and the Voice of the Martyrs (Minneapolis, MN: Bethany House, 2002), 87–88. Bethany House is a division of Baker Publishing Group.

3 Billy Buchanan, "A Total Life Change" in *Encounters with God*, compiled by Kelly Carr (Cincinnati: Standard Publishing, 2005), 131–5. Used by permission.

4 See John 14:6.

5 Rachael's story adapted from *My Prince Will Come: Waiting for the Lord's Return* © 2005 by Sheri Rose Shepherd.

6 See Matthew 10:38.

7 Adapted from Brother Andrew with Verne Becker, *The Calling* (Grand Rapids: Revell, 2002), 125–128. Fleming H. Revell is a division of Baker Publishing Group.